MAKING TIME WORK FOR YOU
An inner guide to time management

MAREK GITLIN has been interested in time since the day when, as a very young boy, a watch that he had taken apart refused to work again. That made him realise that time was something that still *happened* without the 'control' that had apparently been exerted over it by his man-made device. Subsequently, his interest in sensory deprivation and its effect on a person's ability to cope physiologically and psychologically without a time piece to mark off the passing hours confirmed his belief that we have mostly stopped listening and responding to our *innate* sense of time, and have become over-regulated bondsmen of the clock.

Marek is a human resource development consultant with London-based Marketing Improvements Learning Limited, a member of Marketing Improvements Group PLC, the UK's largest independent marketing and training consultancy.

He is married with two children and lives in Northamptonshire.

Overcoming Common Problems Series

Overcoming Common Problems Series

Feverfew
A traditional herbal remedy for migraine and arthritis
DR STEWART JOHNSON

Fight Your Phobia and Win
DAVID LEWIS

Getting Along with People
DIANNE DOUBTFIRE

Goodbye Backache
DR DAVID IMRIE WITH COLLEEN DIMSON

Helping Children Cope with Divorce
ROSEMARY WELLS

Helping Children Cope with Grief
ROSEMARY WELLS

How to be a Successful Secretary
SUE DYSON AND STEPHEN HOARE

How to Be Your Own Best Friend
DR PAUL HAUCK

How to Control your Drinking
DRS W. MILLER AND R. MUNOZ

How to Cope with Stress
DR PETER TYRER

How to Cope with Tinnitus and Hearing Loss
DR ROBERT YOUNGSON

How to Cope with Your Child's Allergies
DR PAUL CARSON

How to Cure Your Ulcer
ANNE CHARLISH AND DR BRIAN GAZZARD

How to Do What You Want to Do
DR PAUL HAUCK

How to Enjoy Your Old Age
DR B. F. SKINNER AND M. E. VAUGHAN

How to Get Things Done
ALISON HARDINGHAM

How to Improve Your Confidence
DR KENNETH HAMBLY

How to Interview and Be Interviewed
MICHELE BROWN AND GYLES BRANDRETH

How to Love a Difficult Man
NANCY GOOD

How to Love and be Loved
DR PAUL HAUCK

How to Make Successful Decisions
ALISON HARDINGHAM

How to Move House Successfully
ANNE CHARLISH

How to Pass Your Driving Test
DONALD RIDLAND

How to Say No to Alcohol
KEITH McNEILL

How to Spot Your Child's Potential
CECILE DROUIN AND ALAIN DUBOS

How to Stand up for Yourself
DR PAUL HAUCK

How to Start a Conversation and Make Friends
DON GABOR

How to Stop Feeling Guilty
DR VERNON COLEMAN

How to Stop Smoking
GEORGE TARGET

How to Stop Taking Tranquillisers
DR PETER TYRER

How to Stop Worrying
DR FRANK TALLIS

Hysterectomy
SUZIE HAYMAN

If Your Child is Diabetic
JOANNE ELLIOTT

Jealousy
DR PAUL HAUCK

Learning to Live with Multiple Sclerosis
DR ROBERT POVEY, ROBIN DOWIE AND GILLIAN PRETT

Overcoming Common Problems Series

Overcoming Common Problems

MAKING TIME WORK
FOR YOU

An inner guide to time management

Marek Gitlin

SHELDON PRESS
LONDON

First published in Great Britain in 1990
Sheldon Press, SPCK, Marylebone Road, London NW1 4DU

British Library Cataloguing in Publication Data

Gitlin, Marek
  Making time work for you: an inner guide to time
  management. – (Overcoming common problems).
  1. Personnel. Time. Allocation
  I. Title   II. Series
  331.257

  ISBN 0–85969–611–1

Typeset by Deltatype Ltd, Ellesmere Port, S. Wirral
Printed in Great Britain by Courier International Ltd, Tiptree, Essex

If all you want to do is cope,
something is wrong. Coping presupposes
the existence of a time treadmill –
and that you're on it.

Learning the techniques of time management
is not a rite of passage from young
recruit to senior executive.

Contents

Foreword

Managing time is an unachievable dream, the stuff of science fiction or, rather, science fantasy. No-one can manage or control time: it is an immutable; it moves forward inexorably for everyone – managing director, office junior and entrepreneur alike. (Particle physicists may be excluded: they believe that in some very special circumstances time might run backwards. Regrettably, if it is the case, it will only happen at the sub-atomic level. In our universe, 'yesterday' will always have gone . . . forever!)

What can be accomplished, however, is a better understanding and management of yourself, your tasks, and your relationships to raise the utility value that you can ascribe to each moment of passing time.

In some ways, the surface message in this book is little different from that in much so-called 'time management' literature; but at its core the message is different, for its premise is a simple one: stop consciously worrying about time – there's nothing you can do to speed it up or slow it down. Rather, look inside yourself, know who you are, understand what you want to do and are really capable of doing – and do it. Time will then take care of itself as one of life's constants, and you can get off the time treadmill –where time is often uselessly chased, frequently at the expense of your health.

Marek Gitlin
Marketing Improvements Learning Ltd
Ulster House
17 Ulster Terrace
Outer Circle Regents Park
London NW1 4PJ

Telephone 071 487 5811

xi

Introduction

Getting done what you want done, in the time available to do it, is much more the result of your inner attitude than it is of using one of the many proprietary diary systems; time management tools can help, but usually only if you are innately a systems-oriented and organized person keen on list-making.

Your attitude is what counts: knowing yourself, and hence knowing your capabilities and limitations; subjugating negative thoughts; perhaps having a clear idea of what you want out of life and using your strengths to achieve it; and developing your confidence.

Artificial self-esteem through reliance on a paper-based or computer-based time system will rarely sustain you in the long run. These things are not enough. Getting the most value from the time at your disposal is dependent upon genuine self-esteem in your capabilities and the self-discipline to take on only what you know you can accomplish in the time available. A Chinese proverb provides an insight:

> Besides the noble art of getting things done,
> there is the noble art of leaving things undone.

And therein is the key to the significance of inner time: you will find yourself on time's treadmill the moment you give up the choice to say 'No' and listen only to the urgent voice in your head that says, 'It must be finished today . . . There's no time tomorrow.' If this is the voice you hear most often, you may want to get off the treadmill.

Hopefully, this book will help you do that. But take with you the thought that there are no immutable rules of time management.

1

Taking a Fresh Look

Much time management training suffers from the same inadequacies that afflict management training overall – the triumph of technique over substance, portmanteau phrases and clever quotes over hard facts. The techniques that are so faithfully followed on training courses somehow fail to make the difference – the *long-term personal* difference – when practised outside the isolated and evangelical atmosphere of a lecture room. Techniques that are not based on the realities of human behaviour cannot fit meaningfully into real-life, real-time situations.

Training course epigrams such as 'Work smarter, not harder' and 'Redirect, don't retain' sound dazzling and snappy – and eminently sensible – within the self-congratulatory air of a course, but can sound vacuous when attempts are made to apply their meaning.

Many time management courses and literature tends to miss the point: *time management is neither a technique nor a system*. Like time itself, time management is a biological, psychological, conceptual, and sociocultural process. What does that mean? The omnipotence of our western culture makes it a powerful determinant and governor of values, beliefs, attitudes and behaviour. Individuals can consequently feel compelled to adhere to the prescribed patterns of 'western'-style working and living. Of course, a prescribed pattern makes easy evangelizing a system for managing time: *society expects this, therefore you must do that*. Living according to, as it were, a socially-imposed recipe is to ignore the personal (sometimes genetic) ingredients that make each of us individuals. For example, the biology of two people can make one a 'night person' and the other a 'morning person'; their psychology can make one a 'systems conformist' and the other an 'independent agent'; their concepts can mean one has a finely tuned natural sense of the importance of time and

1

the other has a more *laissez-faire* attitude towards time's passing; and their allegiances to western society and its cultures can mean that one fully embraces its values and expectations and the other exists, perhaps in spite of its omnipresence. If there is a single point to *Making Time Work for You* it is this: in western society people have mostly forgotten the art and importance of listening to their inner voice. Our reliance on material clocks, watches, broadcast time checks, factory sirens, etc. is starkly contrasted with the inner sense of time that today still serves aboriginal peoples perfectly well (though, paradoxically, a watch is often prized as a sign of 'civilization'). We still have that inner voice, sometimes not much more than a whisper in the noise of twentieth century living; but, as the audible messenger of our inherited instincts, given half a chance it can still empower us with the confidence needed to take the best courses of action, escape an imposed 'life script', and be ourselves.

So, how you manage your time should only ever be what is right for *you* and will help you to relate to the world in which you choose to operate, not necessarily one imposed or contrived to fit the idealism of a training course on time management.

There is, of course, nothing wrong with keeping appointment dates and lists of things to do on scraps of paper in your pocket, if that works for you; and if other people religiously divide their day into 'A', 'B' and 'C' time and you don't – but you nevertheless get done what must be done – that too is fine; and if other people allow their time management system to rule their lives (to the extent of only seeing visitors or making telephone calls when the diary permits it), but you rule your diary and do things – things that you can do – within reason when you feel like it, that is fine also. The point is, most conscientious and concerned working people do not *deliberately* delegate or communicate poorly, operate in a disorganized way, procrastinate, or daydream. Mostly, they are as productive as they personally wish to be, or can be within their society or company's method of working and its systems, or can be within their own biological and psychological limitations. How an individual conceives time is important.

If the responsibilities and expectations of your current occupation require you to be a significantly different person from the one you are or want to be, no amount of time management training is going to achieve that particular turnabout miracle: other actions in these instances must be considered first, for what we are alluding to here is a poor match between the profile of your job and your personal profile. In other words, you could be a psychologically square peg in a strategically round hole.

How can you find out? One simple way that produces rough and ready, though usable, insights is as follows:

1. Mark up a sheet of paper into the four columns shown below:

You		Your job	
Strengths	*Weaknesses*	*Opportunities*	*Threats*

2. Complete the *strengths* column with all your proficiencies plus the positive values, beliefs, attitudes and behaviours that you have now or to which you aspire.
3. Complete the *weaknesses* column with all personal factors that either prevent you fulfilling the potential of your strengths, or dilute their effects, or cancel them out.
4. Now complete the job *opportunities* column with all aspects of your job that enable you to express your strengths.
5. Finally, complete the job *threats* column with those aspects of your job that make you either unhappy or worried.
6. Now it's a simple case of answering some fundamental questions, for example: Are there adequate job opportunities

to express my strengths? Do the job's threats outweigh its opportunities? Would the weaknesses I've listed remain weaknesses if I appraised myself by some other job or personal standards? Is it the weaknesses I've listed that prevent me taking advantage of the job's opportunities, or the job's threats that prevent me expressing my strengths? Can I offer more strengths than weaknesses to fulfil the job's opportunities? Does the job offer more opportunities than threats for my strengths? Am I happy to live with the weaknesses I've listed? Are my colleagues or managers willing to accept my weaknesses – because they are out-weighed by my strengths? Given another job, how many of my strengths and weaknesses would switch columns?

Of course, there are many professional sources of career and personal counselling.

If you wish to embrace personal change for the sake of your ambitions or for others with whom you work, or because your performance is variable or inconsistent with what is expected – or because scraps of paper no longer work – then a way to make you more effective is to change the way you think about yourself, your work and how you use your time. However, as we said above, to make that change is perhaps asking too much of this or any other book on purely time management. The change must take place from *within* you. A cosmetic change on the outside, for example starting to use a diary system because it is fashionable, may make you look good in others' eyes but may not satisfy your psychological needs as a self-determining individual.

2

Thinking About Yourself

In your working life it is unlikely that you will consciously waste time purely for the sake of it. The consequences of such destructive behaviour are obvious. On the other hand, you probably engage at times in activities that apparently add nothing to the utility value of your time: idle chitchat with a colleague; leafing through a journal without really reading it; looking out of the window and daydreaming – these are examples of such apparently aimless 'time stealers'.

Then suddenly you snap awake, see how industrious your fellow workers have been during your reverie and, even though your distraction was stimulated by a biological or psychological necessity to withdraw from the task, motivated by guilt you attempt to hurry and catch up the lost time. The more conscious you become of having 'wasted' time the more enveloping that thought can become, sometimes to the point when the worry of having lost time compromises your mental effort to re-focus on what you were supposed to be doing.

The most pernicious trick that your mind can then play on you is to compare yourself with a colleague who, by every measure, is successful and seemingly never wastes time the way you just have. Guilt compounds guilt and perhaps not until you have worked on far later than you would usually, do you feel able to relax, that voice in your head saying: 'Two hours wasted . . . You'll never catch up . . . You're seriously falling behind . . . Work faster, faster: look at the time' finally silenced.

Well, this might be an extreme picture; but as a personal strategy for using time, worrying about time that has gone, hurrying to recapture lost hours, comparison of self with others, and working late just to make yourself feel better, these things have little to offer except, perhaps, frustration and disillusionment. Under 'hurry up' conditions – especially those imposed by others or your own negative thoughts of loss, uselessness, worry

5

–you are likely to make more mistakes. You will be less able to think objectively, plan and reflect before taking action. The days begin to appear frenzied, and the quality of work suffers.

Following a model (or pattern of behaviour) that does not come naturally to you can be a certain way of constructing your own time treadmill. In the end, a person can become intimidated by the apparent lack of time to do everything and thus allow themselves to be controlled. Such a person will be peddling furiously on a time treadmill created for them by other people. A step in the direction of getting off the treadmill is to acknowledge what you are capable of doing and being, and saying no to what you cannot do and attempts to turn you into what you don't want to be and can never be.

In the last analysis, no-one should have more control over your time than you. It is *your* time, and if how you spend it causes you or others a problem there are only two choices: change your behaviour – *can* you, do you *wish* to? – or change your occupation.

To make that choice you must first think about yourself.

Time is not adaptable, but people are. To get a higher utility value from time means adapting to its passage in some appropriate, self-satisfying and self-achievable way. In other words, if you know and care that your performance is slipping because you mostly fail to produce as much as you could during a given period of time then you must adopt new patterns of thinking and working – but only those patterns that are right for what must be achieved, right because they satisfy personal ambitions, and right because you wish to and *can* adopt them. But remember, new time management behaviours alone so rarely turn postroom clerks into managing directors of multinational corporations – without there already being an underlying and very much more powerful drive, ambition, and motivation to be something else and to succeed – that such changes from minor to major are the stuff of apocryphal legend on time management training courses. Time management training will not make of you someone you don't already want to become: if you have the drive to be a chief executive you are likely already to possess a good sense of time and how to use it efficiently.

The process of developing that sense begins by learning more about who you are now and the strengths and weaknesses of your current time management attitudes and behaviours.

The inner time assessment

Introduction

The inner time assessment is a means of gathering information about yourself and how you currently use time. The assessment is divided into two parts. The first part is called the *foundation profile*. It consists of 48 statements about the use of time that apply to any job. The second part is called the *upper profile*. This consists of 12 statements concerning supervisory or management responsibilities.

Please respond to the statements in the foundation profile first, irrespective of your job. Then respond to the statements in the upper profile but *only* if you are responsible for supervising or managing other people.

Completing the foundation profile

1. Read each statement and consider to what degree it applies to you in your current occupation. If you are reading this away from your office, imagine a typical working period and hold that picture in your mind as you complete the profile.
2. Alongside each statement are four response choices: strongly agree, mildly agree, mildly disagree, strongly disagree. Each choice is represented by one of four (Greek) letters: α, β, γ, δ. For each statement, circle the letter in whichever of the response choice columns is closest to your feeling about the statement.
3. Read each statement carefully and think about the response: it should be the one that best represents your normal behaviour. There is no time limit, though you should be able to complete the 48 statements in under 10 minutes.

7

4. Further instructions follow after the foundation profile.

The inner time assessment	Foundation profile			
	Strongly agree	*Mildly agree*	*Mildly disagree*	*Strongly disagree*
1. Constantly switching my priorities prevents me getting as much done as I should.	δ	γ	β	α
2. Interruptions are one of my major time wasters.	δ	γ	β	α
3. I regularly prepare a daily list of things to do.	α	β	γ	δ
4. I put priority codes against all the items on my daily activities list.	α	β	γ	δ
5. Recurring crises frequently happen in my job.	δ	γ	β	α
6. During the past year I've analysed the different kinds of paperwork and forms generated in my job to see if any can be eliminated, simplified or improved.	α	β	γ	δ
7. I've discussed with my manager, colleagues or subordinates within the past month how to solve time problems.	α	β	γ	δ
8. I tend to do the quick, easy and enjoyable things first.	δ	γ	β	α
9. Most people would say I'm a fast starter.	α	β	γ	δ

THINKING ABOUT YOURSELF

	Strongly agree	Mildly agree	Mildly disagree	Strongly disagree
10. I have a list of long-range personal objectives.	α	β	γ	δ
11. During the past year, I recorded a time log of exactly how I spent my time for at least one week.	α	β	γ	δ
12. Meetings are one of my major time-wasters.	δ	γ	β	α
13. It's hard to stay on top of all my reading.	δ	γ	β	α
14. People often have to wait for me, or for work I'm supposed to deliver.	δ	γ	β	α
15. I have to wait for the right mood to do creative work.	δ	γ	β	α
16. It's usually easy for me to say 'No' to other people.	α	β	γ	δ
17. I have a list of work or professional performance objectives that are specific, measurable, and have definite target dates.	α	β	γ	δ
18. I seem to jump around from task to task and often leave things unfinished.	δ	γ	β	α
19. I use a follow-up system to help keep track of work outstanding.	α	β	γ	δ
20. Unnecessary socializing takes up too much of my day.	δ	γ	β	α

	Strongly agree	Mildly agree	Mildly disagree	Strongly disagree
21. I am able to act on paperwork the first time I pick it up so that I only have to handle it once.	α	β	γ	δ
22. I tend to get overly involved in other people's work and I do things for them that they could and should do themselves.	δ	γ	β	α
23. I postpone things which aren't very urgent, even though they may be important.	δ	γ	β	α
24. I can develop a high energy level quickly and maintain it for a long time.	α	β	γ	δ
25. I have a list of all the smaller tasks, jobs and assignments that need to be handled over the next few weeks.	α	β	γ	δ
26. I don't have to take important work home in the evenings or at weekends to get it done.	α	β	γ	δ
27. Things seem to take longer than I thought they would and I usually end up trying to tackle too much at once.	δ	γ	β	α
28. I can find quiet, uninterrupted time whenever I need it.	α	β	γ	δ

THINKING ABOUT YOURSELF

	Strongly agree	Mildly agree	Mildly disagree	Strongly disagree
29. I've been able to reduce the time it takes to handle my paperwork.	α	β	γ	δ
30. I regularly ask others to tell me how I waste their time so that I can improve conditions.	α	β	γ	δ
31. I often feel guilty about all the things that I'm not getting done.	δ	γ	β	α
32. I like to change and create new habits.	α	β	γ	δ
33. I review my long-range performance objectives at least once every week.	α	β	γ	δ
34. I have to come in early or work late to get my job done.	δ	γ	β	α
35. I always prepare a weekly plan with specific objectives and how to accomplish them.	α	β	γ	δ
36. I usually answer my telephone, even if it rings during an important conversation.	δ	γ	β	α
37. My desk or work area is rather cluttered and I feel it should be neater.	δ	γ	β	α
38. I save things up and handle several things in one visit so I won't interrupt others so much during the day.	α	β	γ	δ

	Strongly agree	Mildly agree	Mildly disagree	Strongly disagree
39. I tend to put off things that are unpleasant.	δ	γ	β	α
40. I have a problem handling stress, tension or anxiety.	δ	γ	β	α
41. I clearly understand the purpose or intended results of all my activities.	α	β	γ	δ
42. I usually start my working day with coffee, conversation or reading newspapers or business journals.	δ	γ	β	α
43. I often fail to tackle first things first, or to work on the basis of what's most important.	δ	γ	β	α
44. Ineffective communication is one of my major time-wasters.	δ	γ	β	α
45. I regularly use a dictating machine to generate my letters, memos, reports and other paperwork that I must prepare, or I type them myself.	α	β	γ	δ
46. On a daily or weekly basis, I meet with my manager, colleagues or other key people to coordinate plans, priorities or daily activities.	α	β	γ	δ

12

	Strongly agree	Mildly agree	Mildly disagree	Strongly disagree
47. It takes pressure or an approaching deadline to get me started on a difficult or complex project.	δ	γ	β	α
48. I don't have enough time for family, friends or other important parts of my life.	δ	γ	β	α

5. Now stop. Are you satisfied with your responses?
6. If you manage or supervise other people, please complete now the 12 statements in the upper profile. If you are not eligible to complete the upper profile, please turn to instruction 8 (page 15) on scoring.

The inner time assessment	Upper profile			
	Strongly agree	Mildly agree	Mildly disagree	Strongly disagree
49. I'm involved in too many details, and tend to create bottlenecks or slow down the work of my staff.	δ	γ	β	α
50. After all my meetings, I follow-up to make sure assigned actions are completed on time.	α	β	γ	δ
51. I have a definite plan for developing my subordinates so that I can delegate more things to them.	α	β	γ	δ

13

	Strongly agree	Mildly agree	Mildly disagree	Strongly disagree
52. When I call a meeting I usually do not write out the specific purpose or prepare an agenda.	δ	γ	β	α
53. I meet with my key staff every week to coordinate weekly objectives, plans and priorities.	α	β	γ	δ
54. It's faster and easier to do many things myself rather than to delegate them.	δ	γ	β	α
55. I review daily objectives and priorities each morning with my secretary or other key people.	α	β	γ	δ
56. I often forget to follow up or check on things I've delegated.	δ	γ	β	α
57. Meetings I call start on time, stay on time and stop on time.	α	β	γ	δ
58. I don't analyse and plan things very well before I assign jobs to others.	δ	γ	β	α
59. My meetings aren't very well organized and we don't accomplish as much as we should.	δ	γ	β	α
60. Each of my subordinates knows the objectives for our unit and his or her role in achieving them.	α	β	γ	δ

7. Now stop. Are you satisfied with your responses?
8. Scoring the foundation and upper profiles.
   (a) The foundation profile
      (i)   Add up the total number of times each letter – α, β, γ, δ – was circled in statements 1–48.
      (ii) Write each total against its equivalent letter in the How many? column in the foundation score box. This column must add up to 48.
      (iii) Multiply each figure in the How many? column by the factor shown in the X column, and write the results in the Total points column.
      (iv) Add together all the figures in the Total points column to give your foundation profile score.

Foundation score box			
Letter	How many?	X	Total points
α		4	
β		3	
γ		2	
δ		1	

Foundation profile score **48**

   (b) The upper profile.
      Complete the upper score box from statements 49–60 in exactly the same way as you completed the foundation score box.

Upper score box			
Letter	*How many?*	*X*	*Total points*
α		4	
β		3	
γ		2	
δ		1	
Upper profile score **48**			

9. To arrive at your combined profile score, add together your foundation and upper profile scores. (*Note*: If you did not complete statements 49–60, omit this step.)

Combined score box
Foundation profile score
Upper profile score
Combined profile score

Before continuing with the interpretation of your scores, go over statements 1–48 again – and statements 49–60 if you completed them – only this time, read them not as statements that you must answer but as statements that contain clues which might help you to use your time more efficiently. For example, statement 1 contains the clue that task priorities should be set and not changed (without good reason) to achieve performance expectations.

THINKING ABOUT YOURSELF

You may wish to identify the clues and the actions from the other statements, and record your thoughts below.

Statement number	Clue to using time more efficiently	Action
1	*Task priorities*	*Set and adhere to them*
2		
3		
4		
5		
6		
7		
8		
9		
10		
11		
12		
13		
14		
15		
16		
17		
18		
19		
20		
21		
22		
23		
24		

Statement number	Clue to using time more efficiently	Action
25	_____	_____
26	_____	_____
27	_____	_____
28	_____	_____
29	_____	_____
30	_____	_____
31	_____	_____
32	_____	_____
33	_____	_____
34	_____	_____
35	_____	_____
36	_____	_____
37	_____	_____
38	_____	_____
39	_____	_____
40	_____	_____
41	_____	_____
42	_____	_____
43	_____	_____
44	_____	_____
45	_____	_____
46	_____	_____
47	_____	_____
48	_____	_____
49	_____	_____
50	_____	_____

Statement number	Clue to using time more efficiently	Action
51	_____	_____
52	_____	_____
53	_____	_____
54	_____	_____
55	_____	_____
56	_____	_____
57	_____	_____
58	_____	_____
59	_____	_____
60	_____	_____

Within both sets of statements (1–48 and 49–60) clues were repeated. You may have nevertheless derived a list of clues and actions similar to that shown below, where clues and actions have been consolidated. (This list is reproduced in an amended form as a Personal Action Plan in the Appendix at the end of this book.)

Statements 1–48

Clues	Actions	Personal strength	I choose to do this
Task priorities	Set and adhere to them	☐	☐
Interruptions (from people and the telephone)	Reduce them	☐	☐
Daily 'to do' list	Write one	☐	☐

THINKING ABOUT YOURSELF

Clues	Actions	Personal strength	I choose to do this
Crises	Minimize as far as possible by better forward planning	☐	☐
Paperwork	Analyse to justify its need	☐	☐
	Either eliminate, simplify, or improve	☐	☐
Time problems (others' and mine)	Discuss with all concerned	☐	☐
	Create quiet, uninterrupted time for my tasks	☐	☐
Time log	Keep one to aid analysis of how I spend my time	☐	☐
Personal objectives	Set long-range goals	☐	☐
Meetings	Question for their need	☐	☐
Reading	Either incorporate reading time in a work schedule or eliminate excess printed matter	☐	☐
Workload	Say 'No' more often	☐	☐
	Don't tackle too much at once	☐	☐
Work performance objectives	Define and deadline them	☐	☐
	Regularly review them with others	☐	☐
	Understand the purpose behind all you're expected to do	☐	☐

THINKING ABOUT YOURSELF

Clues	Actions	Personal strength	I choose to do this
Working pattern	Don't always do the quickest, easiest and more enjoyable tasks first	☐	☐
	Don't put off unpleasant tasks	☐	☐
	Don't switch from task to task leaving things unfinished	☐	☐
	Don't always wait for deadlines to stimulate action	☐	☐
	Interrupt others as little as possible	☐	☐
	Get down to work as soon as you arrive	☐	☐
Tracking work	Use a follow-up system	☐	☐
Socializing at work	Minimize	☐	☐
Other peoples' work	Help but don't do it for them	☐	☐
'Urgent' versus 'important' work	Differentiate and act accordingly	☐	☐
Weekend and evening working	Eliminate it	☐	☐
	Plan each day	☐	☐
	Make more time for your home life	☐	☐
Neatness	Tidy your office (filing system and desk)	☐	☐

Clues	Actions	Personal strength	I choose to do this
	Get organized for working	☐	☐
Stress	Seek advice or help	☐	☐
Communication	Improve it	☐	☐

Statements 49–60

Clues	Actions	Personal strength	I choose to do this
Working pattern	Concentrate more on the 'big picture'	☐	☐
	Don't cause a work bottleneck by becoming bogged down in trivia	☐	☐
Meetings	Define their purpose	☐	☐
	Prepare an agenda	☐	☐
	Monitor the completion of assigned tasks	☐	☐
	Ensure they start and stop as advertized	☐	☐
	Regularly meet with your people to coordinate objectives, plans, and priorities	☐	☐
Delegation	Develop your people to handle delegated work	☐	☐
	Plan delegated work before assigning it	☐	☐
	Monitor completion of delegated work	☐	☐

Alongside each of the actions in the above list are two boxes. You may now like to tick any in the first column that are the same as or approximate the strengths you listed in the excercise explained on page 3; and you may like to tick any in the second column that stand for what you wish to, and personally can do something about. However, don't tick a box in the second column just because *other people* have told you that that is an action you should take: being told to complete a daily 'to do' list, for example, might become a daily cross to bear if you are not naturally a list-maker; similarly, you might keep your office or desk tidier for a short while after being advised to do so, but if *you* feel comfortable working in clutter – and it *does not stop you fulfilling your responsibilities* – there's no value in using your time to create an appearance that you have no interest in sustaining. Don't dissipate your energy on time management techniques that are likely to be no more than five minute novelties.

And again, most time management literature emphasizes how life goals are the precursor of the better utilization of time: what you want to do or to become dictates what you should be doing now, hence the activities on which you should be spending your time. Goals *are* important: aims, targets offer a focus and minimize abstract aimlessness and the tendency otherwise to be prey to serendipity. Successful business people are frequently characterized by their unswerving pursuit of a clear vision of what they want to become, to achieve in business and life. But if you are not a 'life goals' person, devising them will probably not make you a better time manager today. Unless you personally feel the need to define an end point and a 'grand plan' – and you have the intrinsic motivation and incipient singleminded energy to pursue it – it is far more important that you develop a sense-experience consciousness of day-to-day time, and the impact made upon your use of it by your biology, psychology, and adherence to sociocultural norms. The point being, as was stated before, it is unlikely that in business you will overtly waste time simply for the sake of consciously wasting it: for you, those occasional non-task activities (daydreaming, socializing) might be very necessary because they satisfy inner needs. To deny inner needs too frequently for the sake of an idealistic and 'external' time management model could become personally destructive.

Managing time is a personal philosophy, one that already permeates your career ambitions to the extent that you may *intuitively* feel you either wish to and must make better use of time, or that you feel you are doing as much with your time as you want. Don't change from one philosophy to the other simply because someone else (or a book) tells you to. The change will probably not last, because in these circumstances it will not be born or nurtured from within. That 'intuition' telling you whether you should work differently is the 'sound' of your inner voice, the 'audible' manifestation of your biological and psychological drives that respond most powerfully to Man's five fundamental needs: to survive, to be secure, to give and receive love, to satisfy one's ego, and to create self-fulfilment.

Interpreting your profile scores

The interpretation of your profile scores will be completed in two stages. Stage one is a basic interpretation that offers a number of broad ideas to help anyone utilize their time overall more efficiently – if they want to.

Stage two – presented in the next chapter, and for which a further assessment is required – offers specific ideas to help you utilize your time more efficiently – again, if that is what you want.

Stage one

Foundation profile score

Your score on this profile represents conditions as they exist now. It is a snapshot. It is not predictive; that is, it does not define what you will be or do in the future. In this there are no absolute 'right' or 'wrong' scores, for rightness and wrongness can only be determined within the contexts of your present work and your personal philosophy.

Your total foundation profile score can be found below. The

higher your score, the more efficiently – according to a theoretically ideal model – you use your time now.

Total foundation profile score	Time utilization level
48–67	I
68–96	II
97–144	III
145–173	IV
174–192	V

Your *strongest* points are those statements against which you circled the letter α. Your secondary strengths are those statements against which you circled the letter β. Your *weakest* points are those statements against which you circled either γ or δ.

In your efforts to enhance your sense and use of time, don't try to change all your behaviours at once. Concentrate first on the areas of greatest significance to your job or your life. These will not necessarily be where you scored lowest. Concentrate also on those areas that *you* can control.

Upper profile score

Your total upper profile score can be found below. Again, the higher your score, the more efficiently you use your managerial/supervisory time now.

Total upper profile score	Time utilization level
12–17	I
18–24	II
25–36	III
37–43	IV
44–48	V

As a manager or supervisor, you have a significant impact on how your people use their time. A high foundation profile score does not necessarily mean a higher upper profile score – as might be your own case: you might be evaluated by different time utilization levels. Look for relationships between your responses to the two sets of statements. Shortcomings in your foundation profile may be preventing better performance in your management tasks. Similarly, shortcomings in your upper profile (those statements against which you circled γ or δ) may be preventing your people improving their own utilization of time.

Combined profile score

Your combined score can be found in the following:

Total combined profile score	Time utilization level
60–84	I
85–120	II
121–180	III
181–216	IV
217–240	V

Again, the higher the score the better (though better only from the point of view of a theoretical expert model); it might not be 'better' for you. There is order *and* disorder in all natural things. Striving for what might be an unobtainable consistent order in everything you do is, perhaps, another way of creating your own time treadmill.

No change will take place without the *desire* to change. Desire is the key to how much more efficiently you want to use your time: no desire, no change; high desire, the higher will be the utility value that you can ascribe to your use of time.

Change is largely a voluntary effort. No one can force you to use your time differently. But you should note that some of your habits could be self-defeating and some self-reinforcing (your weaknesses and strengths within your current occupation); and as other people may well be affected by your behaviour, you should note also a possible need to change for others' sake, if not your own.

To assist your efforts to eliminate self-defeating habits and replace them with self-reinforcing habits (assuming you want to continue or advance in your current occupation), you may wish to try the following ideas:

1. *Identify the habit you want to change*. In order to pinpoint the precise behaviour that you wish to change, you will have to analyse all your behaviours and the situations that stimulate them. Carefully examine your attitudes and the bases for them to see if any are unreasonably holding you back from achieving the change you desire. The more you know about what you do, when you do it, and why you do it, the easier it will be for you to identify habits that are detrimental.

2. *Define precisely the new habit you wish to develop*. Draw a line down the middle of a sheet of paper from top to bottom. On the left-hand side, describe the new behaviour you plan to adopt and, on the right-hand side, the situations for when it will be most appropriate. Gather whatever information or resources you need to implement the change and visualize yourself in your new role. To succeed, that vision must become your inner 'voice'.

3. *Begin the new behaviour as strongly as possible*. Tell everyone you can about the new habit you want to develop. Set up a routine to go with your habit. If possible, change your environment to give your new habit some 'fresh air' to grow in. In short, do everything you can to develop the strongest motivation possible for engaging in the new behaviour.

4. *Never deviate from the behaviour until the new habit is firmly established*. Many people do the right things some of the time. A few do the right things most of the time. Almost none do the right things all the time. Part-time application doesn't develop good habits. Consistency and persistence are the only way to develop habits that lead to good results. You will be tempted many times to do things in the old way. Resist these temptations. Some people rationalize deviations by saying,

'Just this once won't matter'. The truth is, each deviation matters a great deal. Every time you deviate you must start again. (Think how many times you have heard people – yourself? – say, I'll start my diet on Monday!)

5. *Use every opportunity to practise the new behaviour*. No matter how strongly you are committed to a new habit, it will not become yours until you actually use the new behaviour. Seek out opportunities to use it. Arrange your life so you adopt the new behaviour more frequently than normal. Do everything you can to practise the new behaviour until it becomes a habit.

In this chapter we have emphasized the 'individual' nature of time: the desire to raise its utility value is, in the last analysis, your choice. However, we have said also that if the way you work causes yourself or others a problem – it impedes you or them fulfilling job responsibilities – you may need to consider an alternative. The inner time assessment resulted in data that will help you create an alternative way of thinking, working, and relating.

All the events in your working life are related, however tenuously: none stand as isolated events. A change in one action will have a repercussion elsewhere and, given that time transcends everything, it follows that your behaviour will affect more than your own time.

This is never more true than when you are responsible for one or more elements of a team-managed project. As one in a team of people, there will be a time when the project's progress and momentum will advance or falter by your actions. The relationships, ways of working, and channels of communication that emerge during a team venture help to define the task's boundaries and an individual's responsibilities; and most obviously during team undertakings, patterns of involvement can be identified: that is, the interrelatedness of people and actions can be split-out into 'blocks' of principal behaviours.

Thinking in this way – in terms of patterns – about how you work and use time is the subject of Chapter 3.

3

Thinking About How You Work

In the last chapter we provided a list of better time utilization clues and actions. This was a general list, in the sense that the clues were not differentiated into specific categories or patterns of behaviour.

To arrive at that differentiation you must complete the second stage: interpretation of your profile scores.

Interpreting your profile scores

Stage two

Foundation profile, Statements 1–48

The 48 statements in the foundation profile can be grouped into eight behaviour patterns, as shown below. All the statements are divided amongst the eight boxes, six statements per box. Alongside each statement number are the four letters with which you are now familiar – α, β, γ, δ. Each letter has now been given a value – $\alpha = 4$, $\beta = 3$, $\gamma = 2$, $\delta = 1$.

To complete the behaviour pattern boxes:

1. Note that the statement numbers (1–48) are presented in an irregular sequence through the eight behaviour pattern boxes. In the first box, for example, the statement numbers are 1–10–17–25–33–41.
2. Look back to your foundation profile and note the letters you circled for statement numbers 1, 10, 17, 25, 33 and 41.
3. Now circle the values against these letters in the first behaviour pattern box. For example, if you circled letter α against statement number 1 you will now circle the figure 4 in the box; if you circled letter δ against statement number 10 you will now circle the figure 1; and so on.

4. Add up all the values per box to arrive at a total figure for each box.

Behaviour pattern boxes   **Foundation profile**

Behaviour pattern	Statement number	Letter/value	Total
Setting goals and priorities	1	α 4 β 3 γ 2 δ 1	
	10	α 4 β 3 γ 2 δ 1	
	17	α 4 β 3 γ 2 δ 1	=
	25	α 4 β 3 γ 2 δ 1	
	33	α 4 β 3 γ 2 δ 1	
	41	α 4 β 3 γ 2 δ 1	

Behaviour pattern	Statement number	Letter/value	Total
Working patterns	5	α 4 β 3 γ 2 δ 1	
	11	α 4 β 3 γ 2 δ 1	
	18	α 4 β 3 γ 2 δ 1	=
	26	α 4 β 3 γ 2 δ 1	
	34	α 4 β 3 γ 2 δ 1	
	42	α 4 β 3 γ 2 δ 1	

Behaviour pattern	Statement number	Letter/value	Total
Task structuring	3	α 4 β 3 γ 2 δ 1	
	4	α 4 β 3 γ 2 δ 1	
	19	α 4 β 3 γ 2 δ 1	
	27	α 4 β 3 γ 2 δ 1	=
	35	α 4 β 3 γ 2 δ 1	
	43	α 4 β 3 γ 2 δ 1	

Behaviour pattern	Statement number	Letter/value	Total
Handling interruptions	2	α 4 β 3 γ 2 δ 1	
	12	α 4 β 3 γ 2 δ 1	
	20	α 4 β 3 γ 2 δ 1	
	28	α 4 β 3 γ 2 δ 1	=
	36	α 4 β 3 γ 2 δ 1	
	44	α 4 β 3 γ 2 δ 1	

Behaviour pattern	Statement number	Letter/value	Total
Controlling paperwork	6	α 4 β 3 γ 2 δ 1	
	13	α 4 β 3 γ 2 δ 1	
	21	α 4 β 3 γ 2 δ 1	
	29	α 4 β 3 γ 2 δ 1	=
	37	α 4 β 3 γ 2 δ 1	
	45	α 4 β 3 γ 2 δ 1	

Behaviour pattern	Statement number	Letter/value	Total
Interacting with others	7	α 4 β 3 γ 2 δ 1	
	14	α 4 β 3 γ 2 δ 1	
	22	α 4 β 3 γ 2 δ 1	
	30	α 4 β 3 γ 2 δ 1	=
	38	α 4 β 3 γ 2 δ 1	
	46	α 4 β 3 γ 2 δ 1	

Behaviour pattern	Statement number	Letter/value	Total
Acting immediately	8	α 4 β 3 γ 2 δ 1	
	15	α 4 β 3 γ 2 δ 1	
	23	α 4 β 3 γ 2 δ 1	
	31	α 4 β 3 γ 2 δ 1	=
	39	α 4 β 3 γ 2 δ 1	
	47	α 4 β 3 γ 2 δ 1	

Behaviour pattern	Statement number	Letter/value	Total
Life timing	9	α 4 β 3 γ 2 δ 1	
	16	α 4 β 3 γ 2 δ 1	
	24	α 4 β 3 γ 2 δ 1	
	32	α 4 β 3 γ 2 δ 1	=
	40	α 4 β 3 γ 2 δ 1	
	48	α 4 β 3 γ 2 δ 1	

5. You will now have eight totals. Mark the same eight totals on the foundation profile chart below, and join up the marks to form a continuous graph line.

Foundation profile chart						
Behaviour patterns	Total points	Time utilization level				
		I	II	III	IV	V
Setting goals		6 7 8	9 10 11 12	13 14 15 16 17 18	19 20 21 22	23 24
Working patterns		6 7 8	9 10 11 12	13 14 15 16 17 18	19 20 21 22	23 24
Task structuring		6 7 8	9 10 11 12	13 14 15 16 17 18	19 20 21 22	23 24
Handling interruptions		6 7 8	9 10 11 12	13 14 15 16 17 18	19 20 21 22	23 24
Controlling paperwork		6 7 8	9 10 11 12	13 14 15 16 17 18	19 20 21 22	23 24
Interacting		6 7 8	9 10 11 12	13 14 15 16 17 18	19 20 21 22	23 24
Acting immediately		6 7 8	9 10 11 12	13 14 15 16 17 18	19 20 21 22	23 24
Life timing		6 7 8	9 10 11 12	13 14 15 16 17 18	19 20 21 22	23 24
Total score						

6. If you completed the upper profile – statements 49–60 – complete the following behaviour pattern boxes and upper profile chart in the same way; otherwise omit this step.

Behaviour pattern boxes   **Upper profile**

Behaviour pattern	Statement number	Letter/value	Total
Task structuring	51	α 4 β 3 γ 2 δ 1	
	53	α 4 β 3 γ 2 δ 1	=
	55	α 4 β 3 γ 2 δ 1	
	60	α 4 β 3 γ 2 δ 1	

Behaviour pattern	Statement number	Letter/value	Total
Handling interruptions	50	α 4 β 3 γ 2 δ 1	
	52	α 4 β 3 γ 2 δ 1	=
	57	α 4 β 3 γ 2 δ 1	
	59	α 4 β 3 γ 2 δ 1	

Behaviour pattern	Statement number	Letter/value	Total
Interacting with others	49	α 4 β 3 γ 2 δ 1	
	54	α 4 β 3 γ 2 δ 1	=
	56	α 4 β 3 γ 2 δ 1	
	58	α 4 β 3 γ 2 δ 1	

Upper profile chart						
Behaviour patterns	Total points	Time utilization level				
		I	II	III	IV	V
Task structuring		4 5 6	7 8	9 10 11 12	13 14	15 16
Handling instructions		4 5 6	7 8	9 10 11 12	13 14	15 16
Interacting		4 5 6	7 8	9 10 11 12	13 14	15 16
Total score						

The more that your graph lines are over to the right – from the midway point in time utilization level III up to level V – on both charts, the more developed is your sense and use of time in the indicated patterns of behaviour. It is less developed in those behaviour patterns where the graph lines are over to the left – from the midway point in level III down to level I. You may wish to change your actual behaviours in these areas if it is appropriate, self-satisfying, and self-achievable to do so. Don't worry, however, if you feel disinclined to do anything about it: the way your graph line snakes across either chart says nothing about the *importance* or *relevance* of any behaviour pattern to you, your present occupation or your ambitions. Only you can decide if you should change a behaviour.

Far from being weaknesses or shortcomings, your behaviours where the graph lines are over to the left may, first, be leads to new ideas on how to think and behave differently to raise the utility value of your time; second, they are only weaknesses according to an orthodox model of time management; third, you are a wilful person ultimately free to choose how to use time; and fourth, at another time or in another situation what is now considered a weakness may be seen as something else.

Listen to the intuitive voice in your head. This will buzz you if there's a need for a short-term fluctuation in your behaviour, or loudly signal a need for long-term change. This is the voice of your inner self. More times than not it is the best arbiter of how to spend your time for yourself, your partner and family, your business colleagues and managers, and your responsibilities. As we have said before, managing time is a personal philosophy; if that philosophy is in harmony with the achievements of business goals and objectives, all that may be required to achieve them more efficiently is some fine tuning of your time management behaviours. If that philosophy is counter to the goals and objectives, a sea change in your behaviours may be required. That is probably beyond the scope of this or any other book on purely time management.

We will assume that all you wish for is some fine tuning. To help you, we will now discuss each of the eleven behaviour patterns included in the foundation and upper profile charts, and offer tips to enhance the use you make of your time. Note, however, that 99 per cent of these are simply common sense; no system or technique for better time management is ever anything more than that.

Foundation profile behaviour patterns

Setting goals and priorities

The very best managers realize they never have enough time to do everything in their business and social lives that they would like to do. No one can do everything, and to try is to fail.

Doing more things is not the issue. What counts is the *value* of what you get done. The best managers develop a strong, conscious sense of time and objective, and they then channel their energies into the achievement of that objective.

Many people think little about objectives. They mostly respond, or react, to pressures from other people and events. But if you want to raise the utility value of your time, you must decide exactly what your objectives are, bearing in mind that you have a right to personal as well as work objectives.

Well-clarified objectives meet several criteria, described by the acronym **SMART**:

S : Specific   Written precisely as a particularized credo.

M: Measurable Contain quantity and/or quality standards against which your performance (in time terms) can be assessed.

A: Achievable Not so difficult that attaining them is beyond your current capabilities and the available resources.

R: Realistic   Not so easy that attaining them adds nothing to the ascribed utility value of your time.

T: Timed   Bounded by time horizons. Objectives can be short-, medium-, or long-term. Achieving short-term objectives should lead to the achievement of medium-term ones, which in their turn should lead to the achievement of long-term ones.

To keep your attention focused on the activities that are most important – the ones that contribute to the accomplishment of your objectives – you need to set priorities. The more an activity will help move you toward an objective, the more valuable is that activity. The more valuable an activity, the higher its priority. Urgency should be only a secondary consideration when deciding priorities.

All activities have some degree of importance and urgency; generally, they fall into one of four categories:

1. Important and urgent
2. Important but not urgent
3. Urgent but not important
4. Neither important nor urgent

Your challenge is to decide what are the most important things, then to focus on these and ignore the others. When you respond to urgencies and ignore the important things, you have a time management problem – you'll be on time's treadmill. The only way to break the tyranny of urgent demands that seem to fill every day is to define and adhere to a pursuit of your objectives.

Working patterns

Much of how you behave is stimulated by habits acquired through experience. Habitual behaviour can be beneficial in that it enables you to accomplish tasks with little cost in mental effort: tasks can be tackled while you are on 'autopilot'. However, being in an 'autopilot' mode means that your behaviour is probably below your threshold of awareness. This is when subconscious behaviour can be disadvantageous. Merely reacting will not always solve a crisis, nor prevent its recurrence. Purely reactive behaviours arise mostly because the individual has abrogated control of their time and activities to other people and events (important versus urgent priorities). This leads to coping behaviour in which the individual's pursuit of his or her own objectives is relinquished to the force of external factors. In its turn, coping behaviour can lead to what has been coloquially called 'ricochet management': jumping from one task to another, often leaving things unfinished, resulting in personally unsatisfying and frenzied days.

Recording a time log – for a day as a minimum, preferably for a week – is a reasonable way to discover your working patterns. Consciously focusing on your objectives, becoming more pro-active and less reactive, concentrating on tasks that have more than only a marginal benefit, tackling the important things before the urgent ones, developing your sense-awareness of time and how you use it (in terms of working patterns) – can all lead to more efficient productivity. Being busy by only reacting to an unending sequence of events, like items on a production line, leads nowhere (except, perhaps, in circles on a time treadmill).

Time Log

Name			Date	
Number	Start time	Activity description	Time taken (mins)	Priority (A, B or C)

Total time taken (minutes) ☐

Total time taken on 'A' ☐

Total time taken on 'B' ☐

Total time taken on 'C' ☐

Total time involving visitor (V) interruptions ☐

Total time involving telephone (T) interruptions ☐

THINKING ABOUT HOW YOU WORK

Instructions for Completing the Time Log

The log is simply a listing of your activities on a particular day at work. As you progress through the day, log each of the activities in which you become involved, adding a brief description so that you can recall the activity later. Against each activity write in its start time, and assign it a priority code using the following letters:

A Essential activity; must be done today; directly related to job performance

B Essential activity; preferably to be done today; lower impact on job performance

C Non-essential activity; no time pressure; minor impact on job performance

If an interruption occurs, note the start time, classify the priority of the interruption as A, B, or C adding a 'V' for visitor or 'T' for telephone to signify the type of interruption. An example of a partially completed log is shown opposite. You will see when interruptions occurred and how they are described and classified.

Log activities *as they occur* and, at the end of the day, complete the six boxes at the foot of the Time Log.

Use a new sheet for each day.

Time Log

Name			Date	
Number	Start time	Activity description	Time taken (mins)	Priority category
1	0830	Project meeting with CRJ	45	A
2	0915	Secretary – post	25	A
3	0940	Write monthly report	30	B
4	1010	Call from supplier*	10	BT
5	1020	Bill came to discuss project*	20	BV
6	1040	Coffee	10	
7	1050	Phoned JAC re project	10	A
8	1100	Manager's task*	15	AV
9	1115	Write monthly report	35	A
10	1150	Secretary – file request*	5	CV
11	1155	Write monthly report	10	A
12	1205	Call from Phil*	14	CT
13	1219	Write monthly report	11	A
14	1230	Lunch	45	
15	1315	Meeting on GX project	75	B
16	1430	Interview JDF	35	B
30				

* These are all interruptions

Task structuring

Finding time to plan involves a paradox: on the one hand, there's insufficient time to plan; on the other there'll never be sufficient time *until* you plan.

There are many reasons why some people fail to plan and structure their tasks into a workable scheme. Perhaps planning beyond the immediate next task is anathema: they are more action-oriented, preferring to be doing rather than thinking. As a result they adopt a reactive pattern, responding to whatever happens around them. Reacting requires very little prior thought; indeed, planning is difficult to do in a reactively patterned day.

Perhaps they prefer spontaneity, believing that a plan will inhibit an instant response. Usually, however, life is too complex to 'wing it' all the time.

Perhaps they see planning as a complex, time-consuming activity: the time spent on planning could be spent on doing. Of course, planning need not be a complex undertaking. Planning means simply thinking about the future in a purposeful and systematic way, connecting that future with today. It has often been noted that the further into the future objectives can be projected, the easier it is to know what to do today. However, that future point does not have to be very distant for a plan to be beneficial.

What you use to plan is up to you. A proprietary diary/time control system can be a great help – if its sections are used selectively according to your needs. Plain paper might be just as helpful if you are not inclined towards the cost and fashion of a diary/time control system. The important point in the process is to plan consistently.

Estimating the time that tasks will take is a function of experience and practice. However, estimating completion time involves a dilemma. On the one hand there is Parkinson's Law: Work tends to expand to fill the time available for its accomplishment. On the other hand, Murphy's second dictum reminds us that everything takes longer than you think it will. Your challenge is to make realistic time estimates.

You can begin to enhance the efficiency of your planning by starting with a weekly (or maybe even a monthly) plan. This will give you a macro-picture of the short-term future. Without a weekly plan you may not realize there's the potential for a problem until it's on top of you, perhaps towards the end of the week when it may be too late to do anything about it. A weekly plan can highlight potential problem areas in time to be proactive. (See page 44 for an example of a Weekly Planning Sheet.)

Once a weekly plan is completed, a daily plan is the next step. Many so-called daily plans are little more than 'to do' lists. These are easy to write, but can be difficult to make work. One reason many lists don't work is that people prepare them poorly. Their lists tend to be a random collection of activities, many of which relate to objectives, but many do not. They are simply random events that have appeared in people's days. The lists include everything from the key activities of the day to unimportant reminders. Very few lists have any indication of priorities or estimates of how long it will take to accomplish the various tasks. As a result, very few people consistently accomplish all the items on their 'to do' list by the end of the day. Most people complain that they carry more and more things over to the next day. In this case, of course, they can rightfully say that preparing a 'to do' list seems to make very little difference in the results they achieve.

A 'to do' list prepared in a haphazard manner is actually demotivating, guaranteeing the preparer a future of frustration. Seldom are all the items on the list accomplished. Thus each new list is simply a reminder of the disappointment to be faced by the end of the day. This strengthens people's conviction that writing things down has nothing to do with accomplishing them. It is frustrating to realize at the beginning of the day that all your intended work will probably not be finished. So to continue to write out a 'to do' list under these conditions is a futile gesture.

Planning is an attempt to control as much of the day as possible. But remember, you cannot control everything. Many things are simply beyond your control. However, if you fail to control whatever time you can, you will diminish your effective-

43

Weekly Planning Sheet

Before Noon	After Noon
Monday	
Tuesday	
Wednesday	
Thursday	
Friday	
Saturday	Sunday

Example of Weekly Planning Sheet

ness. Whether you can take charge of eight hours a day or one hour a day is, in a sense, irrelevant. The idea is to control whatever time you can control, so you can spend as much time as possible on the truly important things. They won't take care of themselves. Things happen because you make them happen. Planned things happen best.(See pages 46–7 for examples of a Daily Planning Sheet and a Things To Do Sheet.)

Handling interruptions

Much time management literature describes interruptions as 'time-wasters' or 'time stealers'; and goes on to differentiate those who eliminate interruptions – 'time masters' – from those who tolerate or fail to eliminate them – 'time killers' or 'time sinks'.

These are nothing more than self-serving epithets that grossly distort the real world. Interruptions are part and parcel of the fabric of business life, and those who eliminate them may be less 'time masters' than unobtainable, aloof or unapproachable loners; and those who tolerate interruptions may be less 'time killers' than available altruists. Business life and business people cannot be branded in such black-and-white terms.

No-one can control everything (nor everybody). What you do with your time depends on you (a unique individual), your environment (a unique situation), and what you are trying to accomplish (a unique objective). The trick is to accept the non-controllable and control the controllable.

How you differentiate the non-controllable from the controllable is your choice; but, broadly, the differences will reflect those interruptions you must accept – for example, from customers and colleagues who need your help; interruptions that are positive – that is, they help you achieve one of your objectives; and interruptions that are non-productive, in that they serve no measurable purpose – not even one of providing a welcome mental break from daily routine. It may be *impossible* to control interruptions that in the normal course of events you must accept; it may be *possible* to control positive interruptions; and it may be *probable* you can control non-productive interruptions – it's your choice: it's your time that is at stake. Remember, you

THINKING ABOUT HOW YOU WORK

Daily Planning Sheet

31 March 19—			Thursday
Time	*Activity*	*Call*	*Write*
8.00			
9.00			
10.00			
11.00			
12.00			
1.00			
2.00		*Talk*	*Do*
3.00			
4.00			
5.00			
6.00			
7.00			

Examples of a Daily Planning Sheet and a Things To Do Sheet

Things To Do Sheet

Item	Priority	Time needed	Done

can say 'No' and you can ask someone to meet you at another time that is more convenient.

Controlling paperwork

The keys to controlling paperwork are simple:

1. *Handle each piece of paper only once*: as you pick it up to read it mentally prepare yourself to make a decision about its destiny. Your choices are limited: read it and dump it; read it and file it; read it and respond immediately; read it and respond later. And then there is the final option – don't read it, do nothing.
2. *React as soon as the paper arrives*: the more you leave paper to accumulate the harder it will be to work your way through to the bottom of the pile.
3. *Generate as little of your own internal paperwork as possible*: keep written material brief, and whenever possible and appropriate use telephone calls and face-to-face meetings as substitutes.
4. *Analyse the need for the forms and documentation used in your company*: you may find that only tradition and the mind sets of a few individuals support certain items of paper: in other words, there is no sound commercial or logistical reason to not modify or abandon them.
5. *Question who* really *needs to be included in each memo*: the answer is often found by asking your addressees what they did with their copy of your last memo.

Interacting with others

No-one works entirely in a vacuum, isolated always from others. Many people must cooperate if things are to happen according to a plan. Efficient time management is, therefore, mostly a matter of mutual influence. Many people will be part of a time management problem, and many will be part of the solution. Interacting with others can be, therefore, the seed of either constructive partnerships or destructive problems. They key to creating the one and preventing the other is to respect both your own time and the time of others. The more you respect your own time, by getting off time's treadmill, the more *use* you will be to your company and your colleagues; for if you stay on a treadmill created by trying to do too many things for too many other people, sooner or later you will 'miss your footing' and your fall could bring those many others down with you.

Time management problems are frequently the result of getting into such 'activity traps'. One activity follows another; one call on your time becomes an endless series of calls on your time – and the treadmill spins faster. People fall into activity traps when they lose sight of the purpose behind each activity, and when the difference between urgent and important becomes blurred. Conflict – between themselves and other people or *within themselves* – can be a natural consequence, for even the most conscientious and willing employees may well question the value of some of the things they are required to do, and of the wisdom of those in charge. Indeed, it is often diligent employees – especially those who continually disregard their own desires and impulses to appear willing and endlessly altruistic – who can experience an inner conflict between their need (born of insecurity?) to fulfil their job responsibilities without fail or let up and 'robbing the company of the time due it' for themselves. The choice between which voice these people respond to – their company's or their own inner voice – is frequently a cause of personal stress, worrying about time being symptomatic.

Discovering the roots of conflicts will not automatically resolve them. With a root identified, however, the best next step – personal counselling, team discussion, task analysis – can be identified. The goal is to reach a consensus on the important issues, important results, and appropriate priorities for working on them, and the resources that can be made available.

Ultimately, the only way to resolve differences in priority perceptions is to establish a continuing dialogue with your superiors, your peers, and your subordinates. You must regularly discuss objectives, intended results, perceived priorities, and appropriate methods. These discussions must involve a great deal of give-and-take: they should not be a one-way communication.

Effective people discover many ways to develop a continuing dialogue about how to use time best. They find ways to talk about time 'waste' without blaming others. They realize that it is pointless to complain to outsiders about how time is 'wasted' by people in their organization. They talk directly to the people who are both part of the problem and part of the solution.

Top performers are constantly striving to develop a good support team. They realize the value of good partners. And they realize that partners are not just subordinates; they are also co-workers and managers. Partners are anyone and everyone who makes a positive contribution to what you are trying to accomplish. Wherever they work, people are realizing that the success of their organization depends on their working relationships with other people. They are all partners, members of the same team. Their organization will never become any more than they collectively make it. Constructive change may therefore depend on your initiative in dismantling your own treadmill and the ones that you might have built for others to race around.

Acting immediately

To act immediately is usually better than procrastinating if this is simply another word for 'purposeless' delay. However, to act immediately purely to avoid feelings of guilt caused by a perhaps ill-defined inner need to leave a task until later can be the wrong thing to do.

Much time management literature defines procrastination by example: tidying your office when a report should be written; catching-up on your journal reading when customers should be phoned; making a cup of coffee when you should be reading a proposal; putting off your filing when it needs doing; being 'otherwise engaged' when someone is waiting for a decision from you. All those 'otherwise' activities may be the result of an inner need to withdraw from a task: your inner self signals that now is not the best time to engage it, and so you busy yourself with what others might think is an aimless and non-contributory activity to 'prove' to others (and yourself) that you are not delaying for no visible reason. The point is, those activities are not purposeless, quite the contrary; they are the result of the natural ebb and flow of energy and motivation in your life. They serve the purpose of giving you time to think, to recover, to realign your focus, to sort out priorities, to listen to your inner voice, to prepare. It is probably an impossibility to act immediately on all tasks all of the time, and to attempt to do so – especially if you promise others the impossible – can only lead to frustration.

However, if procrastination becomes a habit, to the point where delay supervenes action, there must be a far deeper and more powerful motivator within you than a transient need to stand back, take stock and reassess your thoughts. The cause of habitual procrastination can be anything from a feeling that you are a square peg in a round hole to continually not understanding what you are supposed to be doing, or how a task should be completed. The utility value of your time in those circumstances will fall towards zero. Procrastinating over an unpleasant, distasteful or difficult task will not make it disappear. Dreading and postponing a task may be more enervating than doing it, and apprehension over delayed unpleasantness may so preoccupy you that other things cannot be done efficiently. Once more, we have painted a picture here of what might be an extreme case. But the point we are making is that so-called delaying activity is not a behaviour that necessarily differentiates poor time managers from others. Nor is it a behaviour that needs to be 'cured' with a course of time management training. Everyone at some time puts off tasks until the last possible moment. The reasons why anyone delays are from, on the one hand, quite natural psychological needs to reassert and reaffirm one's own identity within a systems-environment and task-driven environment (by saying to oneself, 'I'll do this in my own good time') to, on the other hand, being in the wrong occupation where delay becomes procrastination as a means of self-preservation.

You are the only person who instinctively knows when it feels right to do something. Putting a sign on your door that says Thinking In Progress is not going to make you creative.

Conversely, remember what we said earlier that getting things to happen right – and on time – is the product of mutual positive influence amongst you and your co-workers. As a caring, mature adult it is unlikely that you will overtly delay simply to be destructive.

Life timing

It has been said, the way you spend your time defines who you are. As in so many clichés there is a grain of truth in that one; however, it would probably be truer to say, *who you are defines how you spend your time*; for you simply cannot do more than your biology, psychology, needs and abilities permit. It is unlikely that this book – or any other on time management alone – will significantly change you from the person you are: you will not become an organized person overnight as an immediate consequence of reading about time management, in the same way that you will not become a *dis*organized person as a direct consequence. What books and training courses might do is awaken a desire and give you the confidence to pursue new work patterns that support the achievement of latent ambitions. Hence who you are – the *real* you – will define how you want to spend your time at work. This will have repercussions on your personal – or life – time.

If it is important to you that you achieve an equal balance between work and life time, then this is what you must pursue; if you weight one more than the other, say, your work life is more important to you than your home life, disregard all that you might read elsewhere that says you *must* achieve equitability – pursuing this is to deny your inner self. It is your inner voice that, if you listen carefully enough, will tell you what you should be doing with your time and the type of environment you should be in to sustain the kind of person you are or want to be.

Upper profile behaviour patterns

The focus in the above eight behaviour patterns has been on you: we have taken a view largely of you as an isolated individual, responsible for no-one other than yourself and responsible to no-one other than your inner voice.

In the next three behaviour patterns we shall discuss your use of time as a manager or supervisor, responsible for others who report to you at work.

Task structuring: individual versus group

Someone once said that everyone, in order to perform well, must know several things:

1. What they're expected to achieve, or to do;
2. How well they're expected to do it;
3. What resources are available to help them do it;
4. How well they did it.

Short, simple and right to the point. The difficulty, of course, is that these things are *not* always known.

Planning is important for everyone, but doubly so for a manager. Not only is the manager's own performance at stake, but also the performance of his or her entire group. Yet all too often managers focus on the individual issue and ignore the later group issue.

In order to be effective, managers must learn to shift their sense of achievement from their own efforts to the efforts of others. As you begin to move ahead in an organization, much of your progress will be based on your own ability to perform. Your ego is tied up in your ability to achieve. When you became a manager, you should have learnt to shift your sense of achievement from what you could do to what others must do. If you fail to do this, you will also fail to do the kind of joint planning and coordination necessary to ensure effective group performance.

It is the manager's responsiblity to see that the work is planned and effort coordinated to accomplish group objectives. Things cannot be left to chance. No organization runs well if planning is haphazard and sporadic. Regular meetings and discussions can make the difference between crisis management and orderly achievement.

Dealing with these issues on a regular basis reduces group-generated crises. Employees feel assured that they are working on the right things at the right time and that their work is going to make a positive contribution. It eliminates bottle necks, and managers who take this approach are not likely to be accused of slowing up the work of their subordinates. Everyone will experience a satisfying sense of achievement that only comes when work is producing results and processing towards objectives.

Of course, all this planning and coordination takes time. And managers, like everyone else, feel the pressure of too much to do and not enough time to do it in. Nevertheless, significant progress demands commitment. Any kind of staff development takes time – lots of time. Unfortunately, many managers let staff development slide to the end of the line, then try to improve staff performance by exhorting people to adopt good time management principles. If you *do* one thing and *say* another, subordinates will follow the example of your actions.

The atmosphere in your organization is important to improving time management in your work group. You and your staff must be able to talk honestly with each other. In a positive, open atmosphere, this is not difficult. In a negative, hostile atmosphere, it may be impossible. Failure to develop an open dialogue with your staff will result in poor communication habits, time wasted in activity traps, scapegoating, organizational politicking, and staff members trying to outmanoeuvre one another.

To determine how you, as the manager, can be most beneficial in resolving group time problems, ask your staff the following questions:

1. What do I do that wastes your time and hinders your performance?
2. What could I do to help you make better use of your time and achieve greater results?

Many of your staff members may see your time-wasters more

readily than you do. Seeing another person's problem is always easier than seeing your own. Be receptive to justified criticism from your staff. This requires a positive atmosphere – and a sense of security on your part.

Creating a positive atmosphere in which constructive criticism – and honest answers! – is encouraged, is easy to create though sometimes harder to sustain. Keep the group informed about what's happening and what's going to happen. Do everything you can to focus the group on results, not on the amount of effort being expended. Help people see how their activities relate to the objectives you are trying to reach. Help them realize that it's not how much they do that counts, but the value of *what they get done*. Think about whether what you are asking for will truly overcommit your staff.

Actively promote discussion *at the time* – don't make people bottle-up their ideas, questions, needs right up to the end of the day. Practice MBWA: management by walking around. Be available. Don't work in isolation. Don't hide behind your title or wear it on your sleeve. Don't expect unrealistic results, but don't settle for too little, either. People tend to live up to what is expected of them. If poor performance is expected, poor performance will be delivered. If great accomplishments are called for, these too will be delivered. Learn to have faith in, and respect for, your employees. But above all these actions, perhaps the most valuable behaviour you can display is to *allow your people enough time to be themselves*.

Handling interruptions: meetings

Ask people about how their time is wasted and meetings will be near the top of the list. Numerous surveys indicate that people spend over half of all time in meetings.

How does the time get wasted? Here are some of the common complaints.

1. There's no real purpose.
2. The objectives are ambiguous.
3. The wrong people are there.

4. There's no agenda.
5. People aren't prepared.
6. The agenda isn't followed.
7. There are too many people there.
8. It starts late.
9. It ends late.
10. There are no results.
11. Decisions are delayed.
12. Follow-up is poor.
13. No assignments are made.

The list seems almost endless. Ironically, people do not complain about effective meetings; they enjoy them. It's only the non-productive ones that make them groan. Meetings are a way of life in modern organizations, as necessary as breathing. It would be nearly impossible for organizations to ever function, never mind functioning well, without meetings. There are at least ten good reasons for calling meetings:

1. To clarify organizational objectives
2. To receive verbal reports
3. To achieve group discussion of issues
4. To analyse or solve problems
5. To achieve acceptability for an idea, programme or decision
6. To train or teach
7. To reconcile conflict
8. To discuss essential information
9. To obtain immediate reactions when fast response is vital
10. To fulfil legal requirements

Meetings also fulfil human needs. Organizations are social structures. Without meetings, individual attachment to the organization is lessened. In fact, if too few meetings are formally scheduled, there will inevitably be an increase of informal gatherings to satisfy both human needs and work needs. The real world is held together by face-to-face meetings. A meeting may provide for social needs in several ways:

1. It defines the team, group or unit. People can see who belongs, and who doesn't.
2. It provides a place or occasion where the group revises, updates, or adds to its knowledge as a group. This includes experiences, nuances of meanings, or characteristics of people and work. This pooled intelligence enhances co-ordination, communication and efficiency of effort.
3. It helps each person understand both the group objectives, and how each person's work contributes to group success.
4. It creates greater commitment to group objectives, activities, priorities. Joint action, taken publicly, welds people together in common acceptance.
5. It provides one of the few occasions where the group actually works as a group. It may be the only time where the manager is actually perceived as the group leader.

Although a meeting can be a valuable event, there is no guarantee that it will be at any given time. While a meeting may be a productive facilitator of group achievement, it may also be a time wasting barrier to achievement. It's the manager who most often makes the difference, who determines whether meetings are useful or useless. However, it takes effective behaviour from everyone to make sure that meetings go well. But, it's still the person in charge who must shoulder the bulk of the responsibility.

Different people react to being in charge of meetings in different ways. Some see it as an opportunity to dominate the group. Others are caught up only in the social process of group interaction, with no need for achievement. And some are simply lazy and use the meetings to justify inactivity.

The majority, however, truly wish to do something effective, but simply don't know how. Ironically, while all organizations need productive meetings, only a handful do anything at all to teach managers how to have productive meetings. Good meetings don't just happen; they must be planned, conducted and followed up.

Of all the major time-wasters, meetings are probably one of

the easiest to solve. And eliminating wasted time in meetings will probably do more good for more people at one time than solving almost any other time-waster. It will take a little effort on your part, but the rewards are especially attractive. Here is one place where you, and others, can easily get more done, in less time, with better results. How?

Preparation

In step-wise fashion, the preparation needs are as follows:

1. Decide the objectives:
   (a) what is the objective of the meeting?
   (b) how does it relate to other meetings or events?
   (c) what level of understanding is required?
2. Analyse the topic:
   (a) decide on a logical sequence;
   (b) has this got a 'beginning', 'middle' and 'end'?
3. Subdivide the sequence:
   (a) divide the logical sequence using appropriate headings;
   (b) assess the ground to be covered under each heading;
4. Plan the introduction:
   (a) what is the knowledge and experience of the group?
   (b) how can their past experience be related to the topic?
   (c) what is the best way to introduce the logical sequence and the headings?
5. Prepare the discussion:
   (a) write out the headings;
   (b) anticipate discussion;
   (c) prepare suitable questions to stimulate discussion;
   (d) prepare own notes and views for guidance;
   (e) decide how particular points can be illustrated using visual material, demonstrations, role-playing, case studies;
   (f) arrange a group seating plan which will ensure free discussion by allowing eye-contact between all members;
   (g) prepare headings on a flip chart or overhead transparency; or hand out a checklist for the group to follow. (See page 62 for an example of a Meeting Planning Sheet.)

Leading and handling the discussion

1. The point will arrive when all around the table are looking to you for an opening. How you do this, and what you say may well set the tone for the whole proceedings. If it is suitable to use a joke to put everyone at their ease and emphasize the informality of the meeting, this is perfectly acceptable provided it does not become in itself an invitation to everyone else to do likewise. After the group has responded to the story, regain their attention and begin. It must be a definite beginning. It will lessen the impact of your opening remarks if you alone know that the session has begun, everyone else 'drifting in' as the message slowly filters round the table that proceedings have started.

2. Always use a carefully planned introduction. Keep it as brief as possible, but ensure that you give a general outline of the whole topic to be discussed. And remember to tell the group what the object of the discussion is, what goal the group should aim for. It is not always sufficient to rely on the title appearing at the top of the agenda – this can often be interpreted flexibly.

3. End the introduction with a general question to the group as a whole, designed to open the discussions, under the first heading on your agenda.

4. When you have asked your first question wait for the discussion to start.

5. At all times you should ensure that everyone understands the discussion.

6. Involve everyone in the group and divert the discussion when necessary.

7. In most groups there will be a 'hogger' and someone who keeps silent. There will be times when you will meet a 'hogger' who will not allow his or her colleagues to contribute. Under these circumstances several gentle techniques can help:

   (a) Make a friendly joke at his or her expense.
   (b) Ask another member of the group what he or she thinks of the 'hogger' and his or her views.

    (c) Ask the 'hogger' to write down, but not to voice, his or her views on 'the next three questions'.

But do it all gently and with a smile! Remember, the 'hogger' is very often not the natural audience leader.

The problem with the 'silent ones', however, is quite the opposite. But remember, silence need not be agreement, silence need not be understanding. Contributions from these people can be encouraged by:

(a) Giving encouraging looks in their direction.
(b) Referring to their particular experiences, e.g.: 'I know that John has met this problem recently.'
(c) Asking them a direct question.
(d) Giving them something to do, e.g.: 'John, could you work out the number of working days in the year for us?'

Be careful, however, not to exert pressure on silent members. They may be shy, less experienced or less articulate than their colleagues. The key is to lead, but not to drag or push or propel them to the front. Most group members will lay between these extremes. Obtain everyone's participation by the use of directed questions and by obtaining the involvement of each in commenting on views already expressed.

Controlling the discussion

It is important for you as the discussion leader to ensure:

1. That you understand each contribution.
2. That the rest of the group understands it.
3. That the discussion relates to the heading and division of the topic.
4. That you always summarize each contribution and write it under the right heading.
5. That you summarize the whole of the discussion under each heading.

Questioning. The value of the discussions depend a great deal on:

1. How you introduce and summarize each aspect.
2. How you ask questions and the type of questions you ask.
3. How well you succeed in making each contributor feel that his or her points were valuable.

You should avoid making statements and then asking for an opinion from the group. You should also avoid asking questions which only require a 'yes' or 'no' answer. Neither of these approaches will stimulate your group to think or to understand. Instead, you should ask open-ended questions which demand thought and require a considered reply. Open-ended questions start with: What? Where? Why? Who? When? How?

If answers are vague or unclear, or if you doubt whether either the contributor or the group really understands the point, explore it further by asking: 'Perhaps you could illustrate your point with an example. . . ?' At all costs, in obtaining clarification and understanding, maintain in your questions an open-minded approach so that each member and the whole group (including yourself) 'arrive' at the right conclusion and do not feel 'driven' to it. It is useful to relate each contribution to previous ones and thereby create a structure which builds on past experience.

Using pauses and silence. In asking open-ended questions you are provoking thought. It is very important to allow time for this thought – no particular length of time, but just as long as it takes for one member to respond and open a discussion.

It is very tempting to start talking yourself if silence lasts more than a few seconds – *don't*: the pressure which you feel to speak is equally strong on the group and it is very rare for the first contribution to take more than a couple of minutes to come forward.

Summarizing. After each final point has been made by the group, it is important that you ensure it is understood by all. It is

Meeting Planning Sheet

Date _____   Agenda   1. ....

Time _____   2. ....

People present: 3. ....

....   4. ....

....   5. ....

....   6. ....

....   7. ....

Discussion Points

Action Points

Example of a Meeting Planning Sheet

useful to repeat the point in your own words: 'What Jean has just said, is . . .' This technique not only helps to clarify the point, but it ensures understanding, and is itself a form of control, a milestone in the discussion path by which progression and direction can be measured.

In 'mini-summarizing' a point, try to relate it to other points made, but beware of twisting contributions to fit your own purposes. It can be very easy and tempting to do this, particularly with difficult points, but the secret of successful discussion leading is to build confidence and trust. Blatant misuse of your position will destroy both; so summarize fairly, objectively and without the use of 'literal translation' or poetic licence to suit your perspective.

The timing of your summaries is important and allows you to structure the whole discussion. You can use summaries to move on to the next heading if time is pressing, or you can delay summaries to allow a particularly valuable discussion to continue. In either case, you should base your timing on the needs of the group and not slavishly on the needs of the timetable.

Interacting with others: delegation

Many time management courses (and literature) include the thought that the best way to save your own time is to use other people's; in other words, delegate – downwards, sideways, or upwards! Imagine all a company's employees, even just those in one department, acting upon that message. Chaos!

Delegation per se is *not* the answer to making better use of your time. Truly effective delegation is a difficult skill to master, and believing that you can master time by shovelling your work onto other people's desks is not only deluding yourself, but possibly demotivating to the colleagues or subordinates in question. Delegating work is sometimes necessary so long as it is not an indulgence to create an 'executive image'. There is no style, grace or dignity in that.

Delegation is 'sharing responsibility and authority with subordinates and holding them accountable for performance'. Managers often talk about 'giving' an assignment. To many managers, this means giving up responsibility and authority. Delegating effectively requires only that you share. You give up nothing . . . unless you abdicate. If you abdicate, you forfeit control and accountability; that never works well.

Responsibility

Your responsibilities relate to the specific results you are expected to achieve. Responsibilities are assigned to a position. Some responsibilities must be performed by the person in that position, while others may be delegated to subordinates. You must decide what to do and what to delegate. Responsibilities of all subordinates are ultimately the responsibilities of the manager. If a subordinate does not do the work, the manager must do it, or find someone else to do it.

Authority

Authority is formal power. When delegating, managers share their authority with subordinates. Collectively, managers and their subordinates should have the authority to carry out those functions and activities necessary to get the results expected of them. Authority should be delegated within defined limits. They should not restrict performance, but must provide for reasonable control.

Authority may be delegated at different levels. Understanding the various levels of authority will help you determine the level appropriate for a given assignment. Here are six commonly used levels of authority. They represent the options available to you:

Level 1: Look into the problem; report all; I'll decide what to do.

Level 2: Look into the problem; let me know alternative actions including the pros and cons of each; and recommend one for my approval.

Level 3: Look into the problem; let me know what you intend to do; don't take action until I approve.

Level 4: Look into the problem; let me know what you intend to do; do it unless I say no.

Level 5: Take action; let me know what you did.
Level 6: Take action; no further contact with me is required.

Accountability

Accountability is the key to control. In delegation, control should never be an afterthought. As responsibilities are being identified and authority determined, follow-up guidelines should also be set to assure successful performance.

You don't want to impede your subordinate's ability to learn and grow, but you must know that the assignment is under control. Control may be varied by how the assignment is structured, how involved you are with the details and how much feedback and follow-up you require. Structuring may range from light to heavy. With light structure, subordinates are told what is expected. The rest is up to the subordinate: when, where, and how the assignment is carried out; plus when and how feedback is to be given to the manager.

With heavy structuring, the manager thoroughly defines the task and how, when and where the work will be completed. The manager may perform some critical tasks and coordinate them with those of subordinates. There may be more frequent feedback on progress and problems.

This story illustrates the point that delegation is not about 'giving an assignment', it is about sharing responsibility and authority:

Somewhere in Army records is the report on a certain Colonel who in his spare time was an amateur astronomer. At some point, it is alleged, he gave this order to his Executive Officer:

> Tomorrow evening at approximately 20 hundred hours, Halley's Comet will be visible in this area, an event that occurs only once every 75 years. Have the men fall in on the parade ground and I will explain this rare phenomenon to them. In case of rain, we will not be able to see anything; so assemble the men in the theatre and I will show them a film of it.

The Executive Officer delegated the responsibility to a Company Commander:

By order of the Colonel, tomorrow at 20 hundred hours Halley's Comet will appear above the parade ground. If it rains, fall the men out in fatigues then march them to the theatre where the rare phenomenon will take place, something that occurs only once every 75 years.

The Company Commander delegated the responsibility to a Lieutenant:

By order of the Colonel in fatigues at 20 hundred hours tomorrow, the phenomenal Halley's Comet will appear in the theatre. In case of rain above the parade ground, the Colonel will give another order, something that occurs once every 75 years.

The Lieutenant delegated the responsibility to a Sergeant:

Tomorrow at 20 hundred hours, the Colonel will appear in the theatre with Halley's Comet, something that happens every 75 years. If it rains, the Colonel will order the Comet onto the parade ground.

The Sergeant delegated the responsibility to no-one in particular when he spoke to his squad:

When it rains tomorrow at 20 hundred hours, the phenomenal 75-year-old General Halley, accompanied by the Colonel, will drive his Comet through the theatre in fatigues. You will be on the parade ground.

Further comment is unnecessary!

In this chapter we have emphasized the individuality – even the uniqueness – of the two factors that determine what you do with your time at work: you and the job itself. The better the fit between these factors – that is, the match between your personal profile (in terms of your *psyche*: personality, attitude, needs, ambitions, etc.) and the job profile (in terms of its objectives, responsibilities and accountabilities, and key result areas) – the higher will be the utility value of your time; the poorer the fit, the less the utility value, for you will feel an inner need to pursue objectives other than your job's and to seek satisfaction of your psychological needs elsewhere than in your present department or company.

Knowing more about time management where the match between your profile and your job's profile is poor may help to ease any conflict. Knowing more about time management where the match is good will probably add polish to the way you already work: in this case, it is unlikely that any traditional time management technique is going to be strikingly revelatory to you; you have, after all, probably achieved your present position by in part demonstrating a good sense-awareness of time and how to use it efficiently to achieve your objectives and satisfy some, though perhaps not all, your needs.

Therefore, we hope that this chapter has at least given you some new insight and the confidence to follow your natural instincts. Your inner voice will be telling you whether you are on a time treadmill or not, and whether what you are doing is what you *really* want to be doing with your time.

4

Thinking About the Future

What now? You may first like to reflect upon the key messages in this book and decide what, if anything, they mean to you and the way in which you now utilize your time.

If asked to say what is the one principal message in *Making Time Work for You*, we would say it's the implicit thought, 'You must be true to yourself'. By this we mean, respond to questions and proposals about how you use your time in ways that you know instinctively are right for you.

Time cannot be changed. In precisely 10 080 minutes another week will have gone – for ever. The question is, will you be happy with yourself in seven days' time that these minutes will have been used to benefit 'time's stakeholders' – yourself, your managers, colleagues and subordinates; your job; your family and home; and your friends – in the proportions that you know intuitively each demands and deserves?

If you need and are willing to change your behaviour patterns to achieve a higher time utility value in any pursuit, then any number of ways of organizing yourself and your tasks better will help. We have described some ways in this book. On the other hand, if a need to change will create an inner conflict, you must decide for yourself whether that conflict is bearable or initiate an appropriate course of action.

What action could you take? The following table offers some solutions, though only you can decide how much conflict you are willing to bear, what to do about it, and when to act.

1. I am rarely consciously aware of any conflict. I choose to do nothing.

2. I am sometimes conscious of occasional low level conflict. I can control it. I choose to do nothing though I am aware that I may have to do something if the conflict increases in either frequency, duration or degree.

3. I am conscious of episodes of conflict. When they occur, they affect my ability to perform as I want or to be myself. I choose to raise the matter with my manager when I next see him or her.

4. There is a constant undercurrent of conflict that is beginning to become the prominent feature of my working patterns. I choose to express my feelings (my fears?) in writing to my manager and his or her manager in which I will also request an urgent meeting to discuss ways of immediately resolving the issue.

5. The conflict is constant with occasional peaks when the tension is debilitating. I feel I am being forced into becoming someone I neither can be nor want to be. I must choose whether to (a) try to resolve the problem from my present position, or (b) change my job.

6. The tension I feel is virtually constant and debilitating for most of the time. I believe I must seek professional counselling if I choose to stay in this job.

7. The conflict is nearly unbearable for most of the time. I have no choice but to seek another job.

The more you secede control of your time to someone else, the less you will be able to determine your own future and wellbeing. Similarly, the more you are driven by outside forces to adopt some contemporary model of time management, when one or more elements of the model are alien to your natural inclinations or capabilities, the less you will be being true to yourself. It follows that, the more you are pushed to be someone you are not and to behave in ways that you cannot sustain the more stuck in a time treadmill you will become.

In the final analysis how you use time will result in either a cost or a reward. So, having reflected upon the messages in this book, your second step might be to ask yourself the question, 'Do I want less of one and more of the other?' You know the answer already. Your inner voice has been telling you, perhaps for a long time. Perhaps, then, now is the time to act.

Remember, follow your natural instincts and then if – and only if – you need to, back up your actions with intellectual justification.

Appendix

A Personal Action Plan

Suppose it is appropriate that you adopt new ways of working or organizing yourself, your tasks, your environment, or others to achieve a higher time utility value. What might you do?

The following is a checklist of possible actions. Tick only those boxes against the actions that are within your sphere of influence; and alongside each ticked box write in a date by when you will have implemented the change.

Ways of Working	($\surd$) *Implementation by:*
Work performance objectives	
• define and deadline them	☐ _____
• regularly review them with others	☐ _____
• understand the purpose behind all I'm expected to do	☐ _____
Task priorities	
• set and adhere to them	☐ _____
'Urgent' versus 'imporant' work	
• differentiate and act accordingly	☐ _____
Personal (life) objectives	
• set medium and/or long-range goals	☐ _____
Working patterns	
• don't get bogged down in trivia	☐ _____
• don't put off unpleasant tasks	☐ _____

- don't switch from task to task leaving things unfinished ☐ _____
- don't always wait for a deadline to stimulate action ☐ _____
- interrupt others as little as possible ☐ _____

Work load

- say 'No' more often ☐ _____
- don't tackle too much at once ☐ _____
- develop subordinates to handle delegated work ☐ _____
- monitor completion of delegated work ☐ _____

Tracking work

- use a follow-up system ☐ _____

Meetings

- question for their need ☐ _____
- define their purpose and circulate an agenda ☐ _____
- ensure they start and stop as advertised ☐ _____

Paperwork

- analyse to justify its need ☐ _____
- either eliminate, simplify or improve paperwork and/or paper handling systems ☐ _____

Time Log

- keep one (for at least one week), analyse it and act on the conclusions ☐ _____

A PERSONAL ACTION PLAN

Note: Your response to this Personal Action Plan will only mean something if you periodically refer to it to check your progress against the dates you have indicated.

Index

Entries in bold refer to a subject heading; page references in bold indicate illustrations.

Publications available from Marketing Improvements Group

by Marek Gitlin:
20 Activities for Developing Sales Effectiveness

Other titles:
Counselling for Poor Sales Performance (audio manual)
How to Handle Major Customers Profitably
How to Recruit and Select Successful Salesmen (2nd edition)
Making Effective Presentations (audio manual)
Managing a Sales Force (2nd edition)
Managing Sales and Marketing Training
Marketing Planning for the Pharmaceutical Industry
Motivating Your Sales Force
Negotiating Profitable Sales
Organising for Improved Sales Effectiveness
Running an Effective Sales Office (2nd edition)
Sales Planner
The Management of Marketing
Sales Management Handbook
The Sales Presentation (audio manual)
Training Salesman on the Job
Using the Telephone in Selling (audio manual)
Making Marketing Work
The Accountants Guide to Practice Promotion
Everything You Need to Know About Marketing

Marketing Improvements Learning Limited
Ulster House
17 Ulster Terrace
Outer Circle Regents Park
London NW1 4PJ
Telephone: 071 487 5811